AMAZING BODY SYSTEMS
DIGESTIVE SYSTEM

by Karen Latchana Kenney

po**go**

Ideas for Parents and Teachers

Pogo Books let children practice reading informational text while introducing them to nonfiction features such as headings, labels, sidebars, maps, and diagrams, as well as a table of contents, glossary, and index.

Carefully leveled text with a strong photo match offers early fluent readers the support they need to succeed.

Before Reading

- "Walk" through the book and point out the various nonfiction features. Ask the student what purpose each feature serves.
- Look at the glossary together. Read and discuss the words.

Read the Book

- Have the child read the book independently.
- Invite him or her to list questions that arise from reading.

After Reading

- Discuss the child's questions. Talk about how he or she might find answers to those questions.
- Prompt the child to think more. Ask: What other body systems do you know about? What do they do? How might they interact with the digestive system?

Pogo Books are published by Jump!
5357 Penn Avenue South
Minneapolis, MN 55419
www.jumplibrary.com

Library of Congress Cataloging-in-Publication Data

Names: Kenney, Karen Latchana, author.
Title: Digestive system / by Karen Latchana Kenney.
Description: Minneapolis, MN: Jump!, Inc. [2017]
Series: Amazing body systems | Audience: Ages 7-10.
Includes bibliographical references and index.
Identifiers: LCCN 2016037289 (print)
LCCN 2016039203 (ebook)
ISBN 9781620315583 (hardcover: alk. paper)
ISBN 9781620315972 (pbk.)
ISBN 9781624965067 (ebook)
Subjects: LCSH: Digestive organs—Juvenile literature.
Digestion—Juvenile literature.
Classification: LCC QP145 .K435 2017 (print)
LCC QP145 (ebook) | DDC 612.3—dc23
LC record available at https://lccn.loc.gov/2016037289

Series Editor: Jenny Fretland VanVoorst
Series Designer: Anna Peterson
Photo Researcher: Anna Peterson

Photo Credits: All photos by Shutterstock except:
Getty, 8-9, 12-13; iStock, 1; Science Source Images, 18;
SuperStock, 14-15; Thinkstock, 6-7, 11, 18.

Printed in the United States of America at
Corporate Graphics in North Mankato, Minnesota.

TABLE OF CONTENTS

CHAPTER 1

YOUR BODY'S FUEL

Listen! Your stomach is grumbling. It's growling. It's trying to tell you something.

What? It needs fuel. It's time to eat!

Eating is the first step in **digestion**. This process is controlled by the **digestive system**. This system is the energy factory of your body.

Your body is a machine. It needs fuel to work. Food is your body's fuel. Your body takes **nutrients** from food. It turns them into energy. It uses them to grow and to fix itself.

TAKE A LOOK!

The digestive system includes many **organs**. They include the **esophagus**, liver, stomach, and small and large **intestines**.

esophagus

liver

stomach

intestines

teeth

tongue

saliva

To turn into fuel, food needs to get small. This starts in your mouth. Your teeth cut and grind food. Your tongue holds it in place as you chew. **Saliva** makes food wet. It also has an **enzyme** that helps break down the food.

DID YOU KNOW?

From start to finish, digestion usually takes between 24 and 72 hours.

CHAPTER 2

TO THE STOMACH

Now the food is a wet, squishy ball. It is easy to swallow. Your tongue pushes it toward your throat.

A flap keeps food from going into your lungs. Instead, it goes down the esophagus.

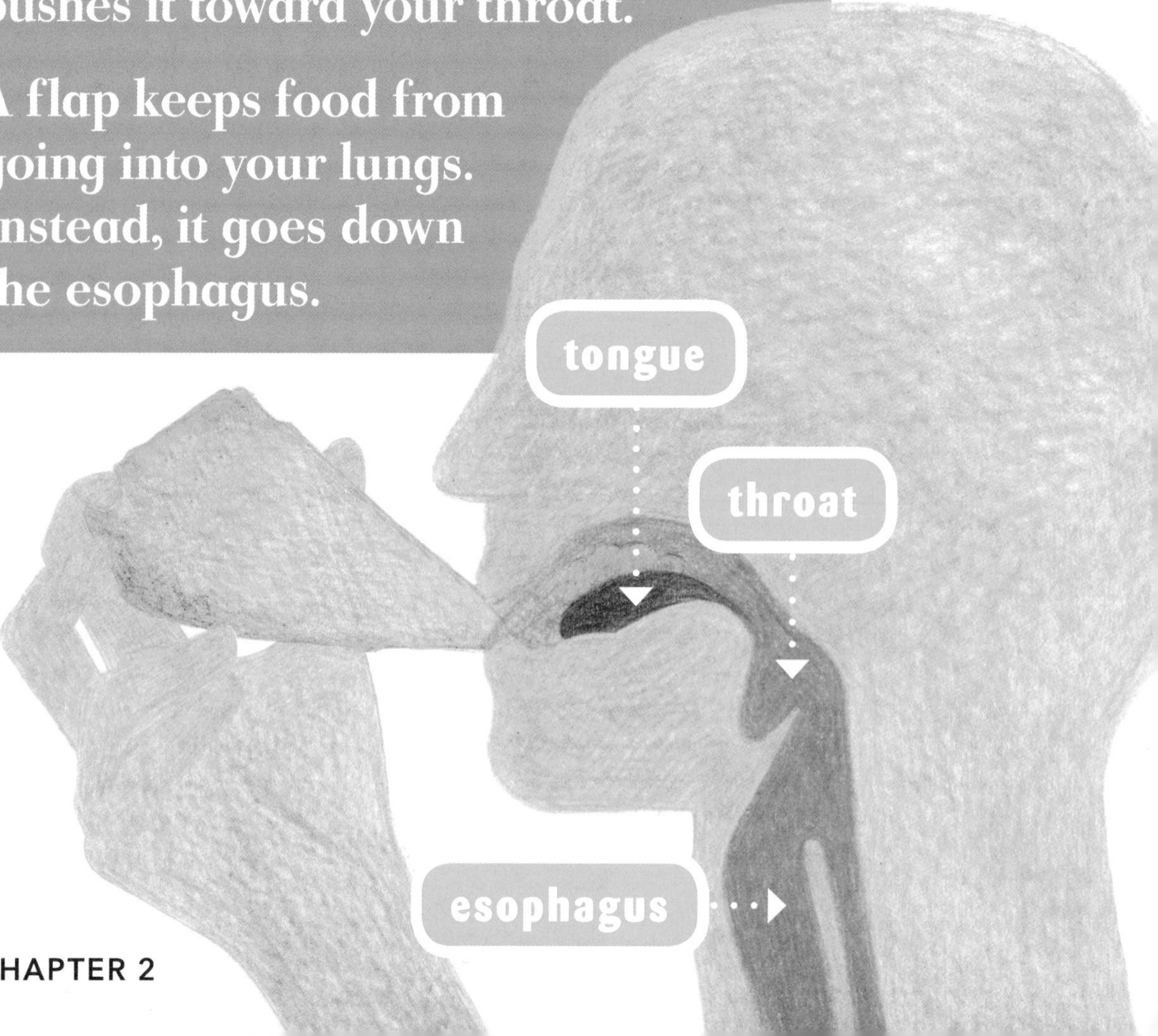

tongue

throat

esophagus

This long tube has **muscles** that squeeze and relax. The ball of food moves lower and lower.

acid

A valve opens to let food drop
into your stomach. This organ
is stretchy and hollow. It gets
bigger as food enters. Inside
are juices. They have **acid**
and enzymes. They break
down the food. The stomach
squeezes, too. The ball
of food becomes a liquid.

The liquid food enters a long tube. This is the small intestine. Muscles in the organ squeeze and relax to push food along.

Meanwhile, other organs help out. Your **pancreas** sends an enzyme. Your liver makes a liquid called **bile**. Both help digest the moving food.

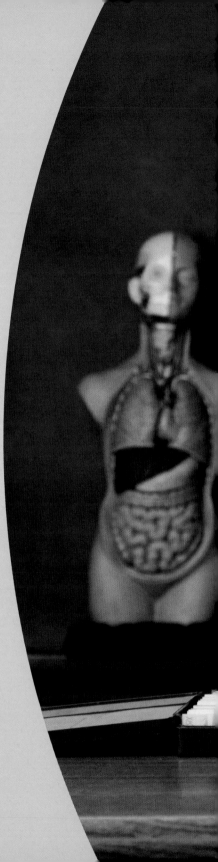

DID YOU KNOW?

Imagine stretching out your small intestine. An adult's would be longer than 20 feet (6 meters). That's taller than a giraffe!

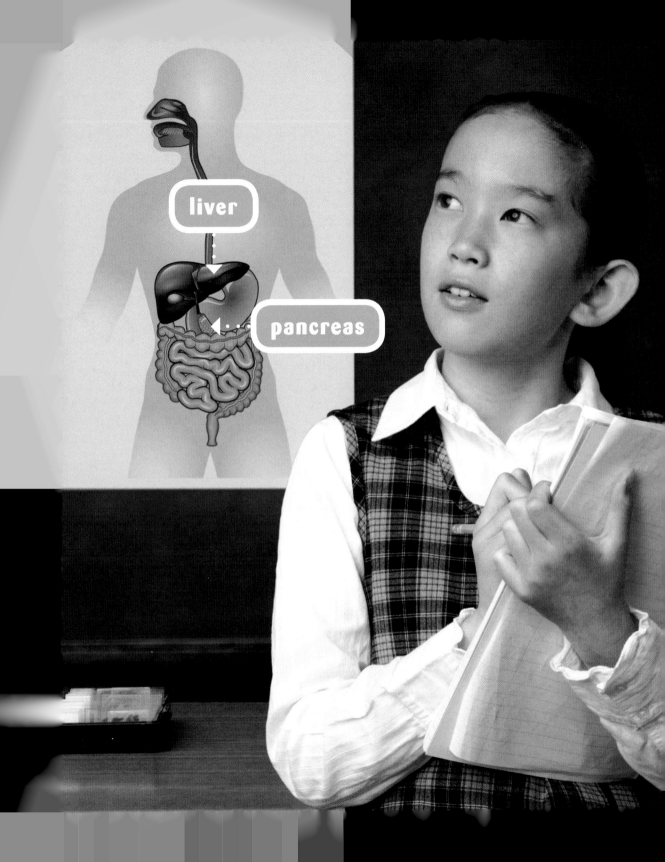

Folds in the small intestine look like little fingers. These are **villi**. They absorb nutrients from food. The nutrients move into your blood. Then **blood vessels** deliver the nutrients throughout your body.

small intestine

villi

blood vessels

CHAPTER 3

WASTE OUT

Now the food enters a wide tube called the large intestine. This organ is busy. Close to 400 kinds of **bacteria** live there. These small creatures break down **fiber**. They also make **vitamins**.

bacteria

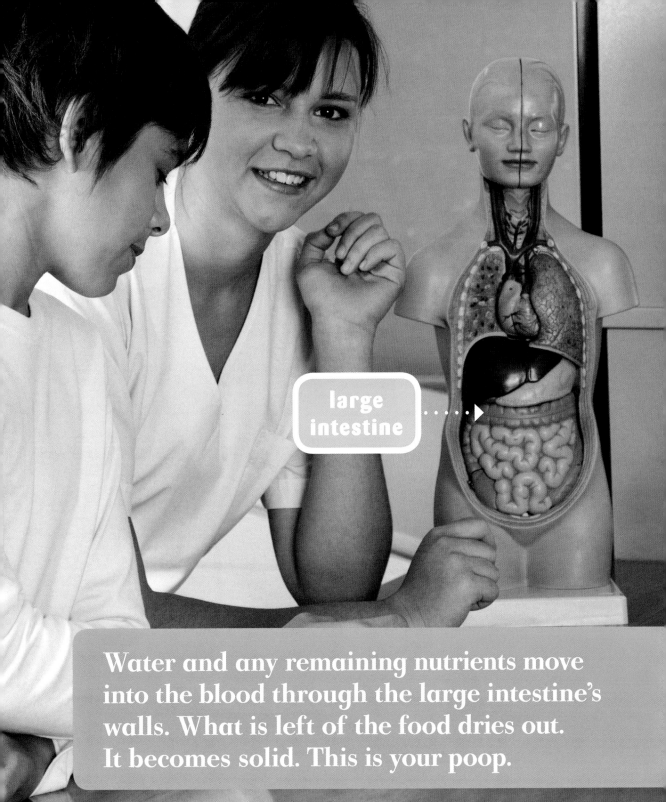

large
intestine

Water and any remaining nutrients move into the blood through the large intestine's walls. What is left of the food dries out. It becomes solid. This is your poop.

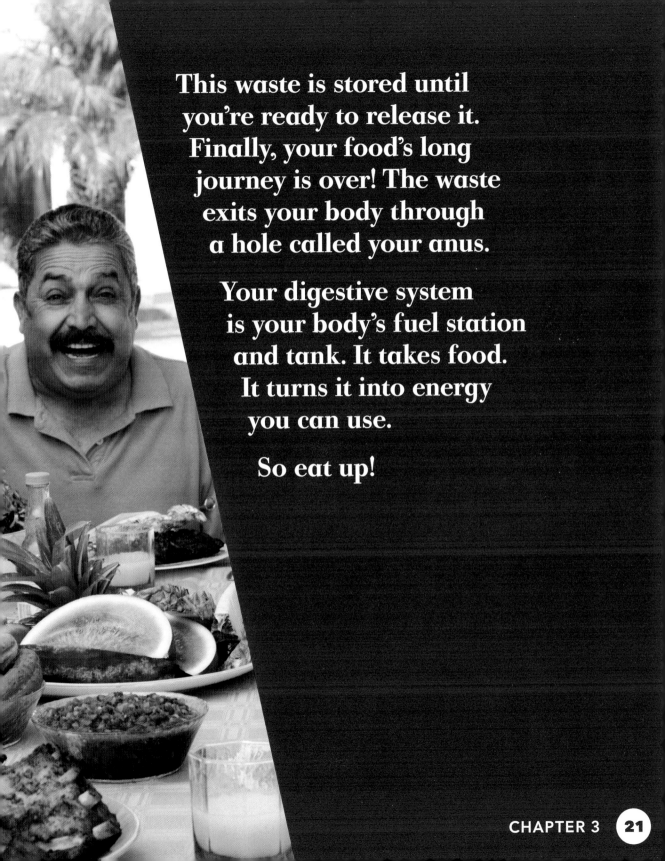

This waste is stored until you're ready to release it. Finally, your food's long journey is over! The waste exits your body through a hole called your anus.

Your digestive system is your body's fuel station and tank. It takes food. It turns it into energy you can use.

So eat up!

ACTIVITIES & TOOLS

MAKE A STOMACH

See how a stomach breaks down food in this activity.

What You Need:

- small zip-top plastic bag
- ½ cup of lemon juice
- crackers

1. **Pour the lemon juice into the plastic bag. This is like stomach juices.**

2. **Break the crackers into a few pieces. Put them in the plastic bag. Squeeze the air out of the bag and seal it.**

3. **Shake and squeeze the bag. This is like the stomach muscles moving. Look at the crackers. What happens to them?**

GLOSSARY

acid: A liquid that can break food down.

bacteria: Tiny creatures that live inside and outside of the body, some of which help with digestion.

bile: A green liquid made by the liver that helps digest food.

blood vessels: Tubes that carry blood around the body.

digestion: The process by which the body turns food into nutrients it can use.

digestive system: A body system that turns food into nutrients the body can use.

enzyme: A protein that helps the body digest food.

esophagus: The tube that carries food from the throat to the stomach.

fiber: Material in food that can't be digested and that stimulates the intestine to move its contents along.

intestines: Two tubes, small and large, that digest food and absorb it into the blood.

muscles: Tissue that can squeeze and relax to move your body parts.

nutrients: Proteins, minerals, and vitamins you need to stay healthy and strong.

organs: Body parts that are responsible for a specific job.

pancreas: A gland near the stomach that helps with digestion.

saliva: A fluid containing water, protein, salts, and an enzyme that is secreted by glands in the mouth.

villi: Parts of the small intestine that absorb nutrients into the blood.

vitamins: Substances that are necessary in small amounts to the body's growth and development.

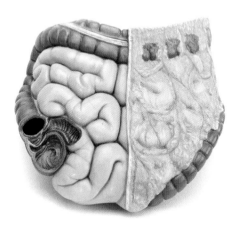

INDEX

TO LEARN MORE

Learning more is as easy as 1, 2, 3.

1) Go to www.factsurfer.com

2) Enter "digestivesystem" into the search box.

3) Click the "Surf" button to see a list of websites.

With factsurfer, finding more information is just a click away.